IT WILL BE
ALL RIGHT
in the MORNING

IT WILL BE
ALL RIGHT
in the MORNING

Rosemary Pavey-Snell

iUniverse, Inc.
Bloomington

It Will Be All Right in the Morning

Copyright © 2012 by Rosemary Pavey-Snell.

All rights reserved. No part of this book may be used or reproduced by any means, graphic, electronic, or mechanical, including photocopying, recording, taping or by any information storage retrieval system without the written permission of the publisher except in the case of brief quotations embodied in critical articles and reviews.

iUniverse books may be ordered through booksellers or by contacting:

iUniverse
1663 Liberty Drive
Bloomington, IN 47403
www.iuniverse.com
1-800-Authors (1-800-288-4677)

Because of the dynamic nature of the Internet, any web addresses or links contained in this book may have changed since publication and may no longer be valid. The views expressed in this work are solely those of the author and do not necessarily reflect the views of the publisher, and the publisher hereby disclaims any responsibility for them.

Any people depicted in stock imagery provided by Thinkstock are models, and such images are being used for illustrative purposes only.
Certain stock imagery © Thinkstock.

ISBN: 978-1-4759-0679-0 (sc)
ISBN: 978-1-4759-0681-3 (hc)
ISBN: 978-1-4759-0680-6 (ebk)

Printed in the United States of America

iUniverse rev. date: 04/09/2012

Contents

Introduction xiii

Part One

My Story 3
My Grieving 7
Turning Points 25

Part Two

"In Denial" 39
Guilt 43
Anger 47
Loneliness 49
Dreaming 51
Feeling Sorry for Oneself 55
A Lack of Confidence 57
Physical Changes 61
Hope 65

Bibliography 67

Review

"Rosemary Pavey-Snell gives us a poignant and, at times, heart-rending account of her own grieving after the unexpectedly early death of her beloved husband. From this experience she then provides an invaluable resource for counsellors and pastoral workers who find themselves involved in the accompaniment of the bereaved. This is self-revelatory writing at its best and will be an invaluable aid to all those who have the privilege of walking alongside those in grief. It will also be a sure comfort for those who are themselves struggling with the absence of a much-loved companion."

Brian Thorne
Emeritus Professor of Counselling, University of East Anglia
Lay Canon of Norwich Cathedral

Dedicated to Allan

(without whom this book could not have been written!)

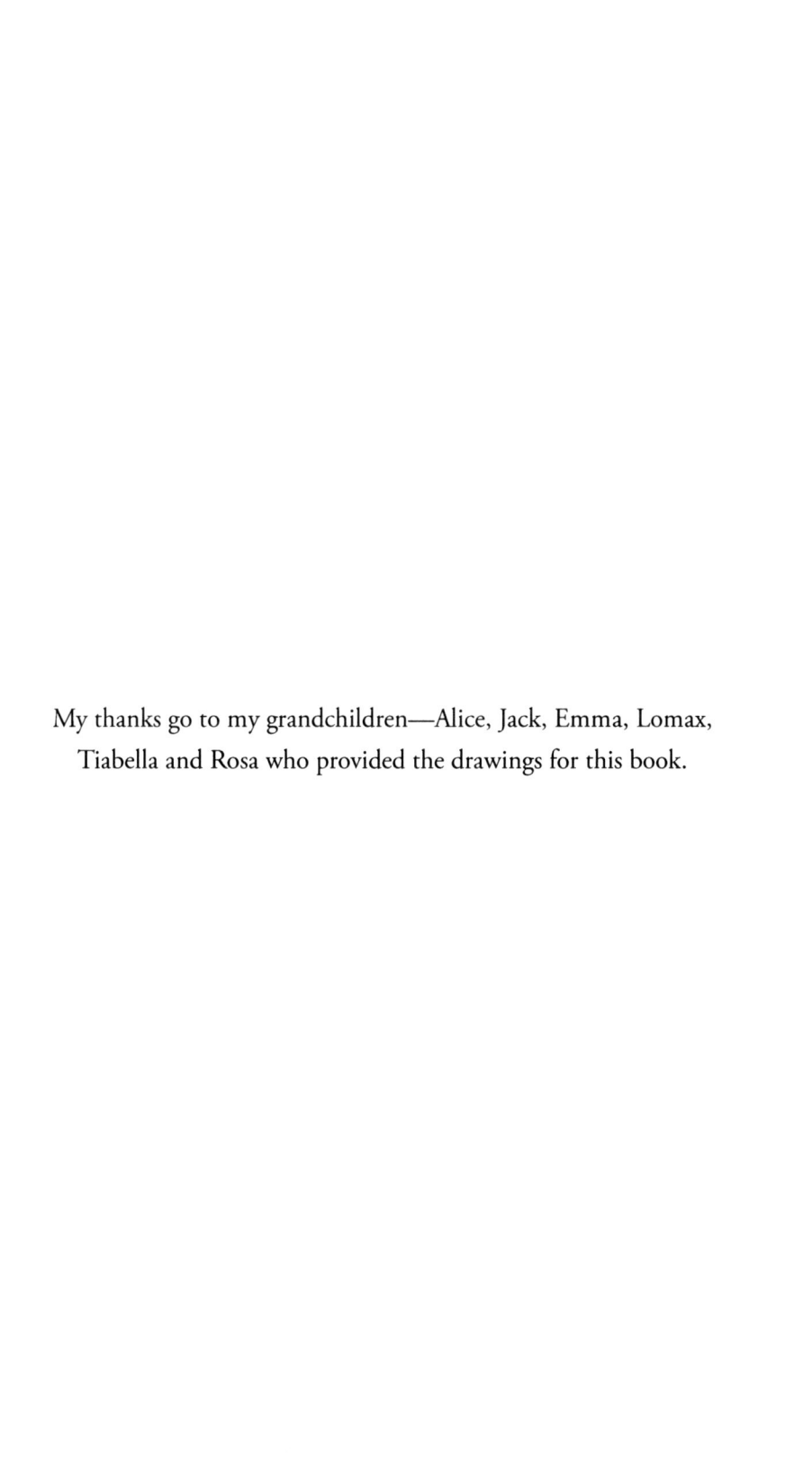

My thanks go to my grandchildren—Alice, Jack, Emma, Lomax, Tiabella and Rosa who provided the drawings for this book.

Introduction

This book came to be written as a result of my own grief which descended on me very suddenly. My experiences are taken mostly from the journal I kept during the months and years following the death of my husband. Being a psychologist, a therapist and trainer of counsellors, I decided I wanted to share my journey with other professionals, giving added insight into the processes and emotions that a grieving person may go through. I use the term "go through" intentionally, as I believe I show my own walk, traumatic as it was, coming to a positive place, allowing me to live in peace and contentment.

I sincerely hope it becomes a help to many therapists and those in the caring world and, in turn, to those who are grieving themselves; particularly the first part of the book, being an account of my story, could be helpful and encouraging to anyone trying to find wholeness while treading through their own grief.

I have sought to be honest in recounting my story so the broken hearted may identify with some of my despair and yet find the strength to carry on.

PART ONE

"It will be alright in the morning"—this was my husband Allan's answer to everything! I was frequently told this when wishing to discuss a problem last thing at night in bed. He would try to convince me that our great faith would solve everything by the morning, whereas I was sure he just wanted me to go to sleep and shut up. He was trying to demonstrate that by faith it would be alright! Mind you, it felt that for most of our lives together he was correct—it really did feel much better in the morning.

This book is written for therapists and those helping people who are "going through" a time of grieving, somehow allowing them to see that it will be alright in the "mourning". If you are one of those people please read on, especially if it does not feel alright in your mourning.

The understanding of this concept was not in the forefront of my mind when I began my personal journey of grief. The ramblings of my story are certainly honest and may show the depths of despair and pain which are often prevalent should a loved one be taken away from us. It can also show the hope that things do get better.

My Story

He was an optimistic extrovert who loved life, God and everyone he met. That I'm glad to say included me.

Optimist—by Tiabella—aged 8

Our marriage began on Easter Monday, 1961. I promised to obey—he promised to love me which we managed to do for forty years—well, most of the time!

The two children we were blessed with are now in their forties. Both have wives, who are not only daughters to me, but between them have produced seven wonderful grandchildren. The youngest three have been born after his death. The last granddaughter was only with us for ten days. I see in each one something of him, but then I would, wouldn't I? On becoming grandparents, our love and caring moved up 20 thousand notches!

Each person who knew Allan felt they were his special friend—that's what he communicated to them and, of course, to me as well.

As we approached our sixties, we planned a move to the south coast of England to take up the business of semi-retirement. Allan began to get pain in his back, with it worsening each day. We believed it was because of lifting heavy things ready for the move. The day before the move, with packing going on in our house, he had a check up with a specialist. The timing was not great but it was the first appointment we could get.

By this time it was hard for Allan to walk upright and when the specialist saw him he gave his decree of "That's not muscle pain that's cancer!" A short time elapsed and then a scan which confirmed the specialist's view.

Our comfortable happy life disappeared into the depths of despair and we fell apart. Allan stayed in hospital for radiotherapy treatment while I moved to our new house with the help of my sons. There was no cancelling of the house move as contracts had all been signed and the chain was ready to go.

One week later Allan walked through the front door of our new home he so wanted to live in. We cried together. Another week later he fell as he tried to climb the stairs. Three weeks later I crawled through Christmas with Allan in a wheel chair.

New Year's Day he entered hospital never to return to me in our new house. He died on January 12th. It was only seven weeks and two days from the first diagnosis of melanoma until his death.

During this time we had some friends, and the elders of their church, who came and prayed for Allan and for his healing. Some church members took it on themselves to pray twenty four hours a day and people were even praying as far away as Kenya and other places around the world. We believed, as much as we could, that he would be healed.

Allan was given bible verses, poems and encouragements from many visitors during that time. You name it—we claimed it! I am definitely not making fun here but I just want to be honest. Love and support were oozing out of our friends and family. I am exceedingly grateful.

I don't have a reason even now, whilst writing this, as to why Allan died much too early.

My Grieving

The first day of grieving I did not cry. I had kissed him after he left me with the soft touch of his hair resting against my cheek. I wanted that as a memory that I would always be able to feel. I still can.

The next day we told the grandchildren. Their pain I will also never forget. Alice who was six sobbed and sobbed on her mother's lap, while Jack who was just four looked on motionless. It was only later that we saw a solitary, quiet tear falling as he asked "will I never see Grandpa again?"

All the family mourned in their different ways. As for me in shock, in denial, whatever you want to call it I made up my pretend world that Allan was still around and coming home soon. I couldn't bear it any other way. I still pretend sometimes.

Someone, who had been through a similar experience, said later to me that it is like nothing has changed but everything has changed. Those of you reading this in grief will understand that, while you go through the motions of everyday life that has not changed, it feels like nothing will ever be the same again.

Each morning I would put the rings he had given me back on my fingers and wonder how he could be gone. My heart ached and ached so much and so deeply. Even physical pain was there sometimes and I thought I was having a heart attack. Anyway, would that be so bad? I really wouldn't have minded going too! "Oh Allan! I just want to be with you" I said, hoping so much that he could hear. I wanted him to know how much our separation meant to me.

The spirit world of God began to be the most important idea to me. One night, as I lay in bed, sometime between the funeral and the memorial, I felt a touch on the right side of my face so lovingly. I wanted it to be Allan. It may have been a comforting angel. Wonderful!

Is there a link between God's spirit world and our physical world? In the ensuing days, I thought a great deal about the two worlds, wanting, so desperately, to bring them both together. I thought of the beginning of the world when Adam and Eve walked with God. I presume this was a spirit world as God is a spirit. Adam, however, had been created with a body. I am only writing this as it was what was going on for me at the time. I am not suggesting it's written in stone.

Can these precious creatures, that have left us, be in both worlds at once? Some would suggest that this comes later but what does later mean in a place where there is no time or clocks? We can try to get our minds and hearts around these notions but the definite knowledge escapes us. We do know, and this verse comforted me a great deal, that:

> "Yesterday, today and forever Jesus is the same." (Hebrews 13:8 NLT)

The other reasoning that comforted was that Allan had defeated death, as his saviour did, and had risen again to be with Him. This, in my mind, was defeating the enemy and his powers. Throughout this time the spiritual dimension became so exceedingly real to me. I wanted it to, of course.

When we are enjoying this world as much as I did when Allan was here we are not as conscious of the heavenly domain. No condemnation to anyone who feels this world is great! I remember staring out of the window, seeing blossom beginning to arrive on a tree and it seemed that if I sat in one place in the room it appeared as if there was more blossom on the tree than if I changed my position to see it from another angle. The blossom was always the same amount and in the same place but I just perceived it differently, depending on where my position was in the room.

God's heavenly world is always there but, if we are in a position to stare at it, we can see more!

I was trying a lot more, in those dark days, to feel the presence of God. I did feel guilty for not wanting God's presence more while Allan was here on the earth. Maybe, I loved Allan too much—more than God. Was that why he was taken? However 'there is now no condemnation.' (Romans 8:1 TLB) I do not need guilt or fear in my life.

I do believe we catch glimpses of heaven, even while still here on the earth, by seeing God's love in others.

When Allan died, I wrote the following poem, which I actually managed to read at his memorial service.

HERE IS LOVE

What can I say of Allan's life?
The many varied aspects of it, as his friend and his wife
It could be his kindness, his laughter or the grace he showed me
It could be his strength or all the cups of tea he brought to me
Each morning—every day of our married life
You want to know what I think of him as his friend and as his wife
I'll give you just three words as sung in his favourite song:
HERE IS LOVE

As we began together along the path you see, he gave me hope
I began to see I was worth a lot. He really loved me
I watched each day as my dearest husband showed me a glimpse of God's love
He cared, he shared, he dared for me
He listened as I told him my woes you see and forty years later I can say
HERE IS LOVE

As we had our family together and he became a dad
He made them feel they were special and if they sometimes felt sad
It wasn't for long as his laughter and fun very soon made up for the bad.
I watched each day as their father showed them a glimpse of God's love
He cared, he shared, he dared for them
He listened as they told him their woes and thirty years later they can say
HERE IS LOVE

And then he became a grandpa and oh what a day that was to be
They were certainly very, very special and they were constantly filled with glee
Because here his fun and his laughter were always allowed to run free

I watched each day as their grandpa showed them a glimpse of God's love
He cared, he shared, he dared for them
He listened as they told him their woes and six years later they can say
HERE IS LOVE

And now in heaven there's laughter and much rejoicing it seems
We look and try to imagine what's going on, what are the scenes
We know Allan is there and he's whole and he's walking
And he's probably doing most of the talking

When together with Christ on streets that have no ending
We'll know God has completed, as He said, our salvation
We'll know He's done away with forever—separation
We will see more than a glimpse of His love
We will bow and worship our Lord in adoration
And forever and ever and ever we will say
HERE IS LOVE

Holding Hands—by Emma—aged 11

The love we had between us seemed like a glimpse, and only a glimpse, of God's love which is always with us and for us. The closeness Allan and I had reveals a small part of the closeness God wants with us. The unbearable pain of separation I felt shows a glimpse of how God could not bear to be separated from us, His creatures. He sent His own son, Jesus, to die the horrible death that He bore so we could be with Him forever. And so it was that I found a measure of relief, at this awful time, by having thoughts like this.

Love never ends. God's love for us, and I like to think the love Allan and I had for each other down here on earth, will also be eternal and made into a perfect love. I don't pretend to understand how that will be, or what form it will take, but I believe it will be forever. Other things will fail and end but love persists into eternity. Eternity is so long and this time here on earth is so short.

God is carrying me and you, who are reading this, and He never has to put us down!

Do you ever have imaginary conversations? I did one morning which went like this:-

>Allan—"It's fantastic in this world"
>Me—"I wish you could cut the grass"

Mowing—by Lomax—aged 11

Faith can build a bridge across the gulf of death, but in this world he (Allan) still cannot cut the grass! I had never cut grass in my life and, although I found a man I could pay to do it at the time, these simple jobs, and how to sort them out, seemed overwhelming. They are accompanied by insurmountable grief.

I want to tell it as it was and not wrap up my negative feelings which appeared to be taking over my life.

Everything was "topsy-turvy". I used to love weekends, especially the warm sunny ones. Now, in my grief, I liked it best when I had to work (Monday-Friday) and it was raining. Why was this? On sunny weekends I was supposed to be enjoying myself, which was impossibly difficult, whereas, I could throw myself into work and, to a limited degree, forget for a while. Looking back, I can see the presence of God with me but, at the time, when grief was at its deepest, even the psalms I used to love reading would wash over me, refresh me a little and then seemed to be gone.

"God is our refuge and strength a very present help in trouble." (Psalm 46:1 NLT)

I knew somewhere this was true but wanted that "refuge and strength" to take away my overwhelming feelings. "When my heart is overwhelmed lead me to the Rock." (Psalm 61:2 NLT) I know He kept me in these times but it felt as if He was only just keeping me. I suppose that was enough.

In the church in which I was brought up, I was taught we should never pray for the dead. I remember arguments between brothers on November 11th. At 11am we were all in the Sunday morning service where we must only think about the Lord and not others—especially dead others! So it was deemed that those who wished to respect the two minutes silence were wrong to even want to do this. I have to say I took on a more Catholic approach and found solace in praying for Allan, wherever he was. Occasionally, I still do pray for him, but not every day.

Yes, my life had been separated from my love, but I lived a great deal of the time as if he was still around. I longed so much to hear him laugh and even snore!! I so wanted to hear his car coming up the drive.

Others missed him too. One son told me he missed his dad, especially when it was World Cup time. I mean football for those of you who don't follow the same. They always watched the games together. The other son wanted him in his business world. He did tell me, one day, after I had mentioned it was a shame that he couldn't get wisdom from his dad, that, of course he did! I remember sitting in a meeting where my son was doing something I knew his dad would be proud of and whispering to him "I hope dad is watching you". His reply was "It's Saturday so he's probably watching Arsenal!"

I do believe those "gone on before" are conscious and have memory. I think this is supported by the "Heroes of Faith" in Hebrews who are written about as witnessing what is going on down here. (Hebrews 12 NLT)

I want to insert a lovely story I read in "The gospel of the hereafter" (J. Paterson Smyth)

"An old county cricketer had lost his sight and it was the grief of his later days that he could not see his own boy play the great game in which he himself had excelled. The son became the crack bat of the school team and used to lead his father to the ground, but beyond hearing the comments of the crowd on his boy's play he got small satisfaction from it. One day he suddenly died. The following Saturday an important match was to be played and the other members of the team took it for granted that their best bat would be absent but to their surprise he strolled down to the pavilion in his flannels and announced his intention to play. He batted that day as he had never batted before. His companions were bewildered. He rattled up a century in no time and won the match for his side. After the applause in the pavilion had died down a friend said to him "You played the game of your life this afternoon." He replied, "How could I help it? It was the first time my Father ever saw me bat!"

The grandchildren have been, and still are, such a blessing and a joy to me, but then I wish he could see what they are like now and what they are doing. Maybe he can. As I sit and write, I believe God has shown me that we will have eternity together and enjoy the tales of escapades here on the earth and then have more and more escapades in heaven! Wow! The best is yet to come. There is no sorrow in heaven because there is no sin "What joy may come from dwelling in His unutterable love". (The gospel of the hereafter)

One day I felt my hand being held very tightly and thought I heard "step out, even into the unknown". We can think of "the unknown" as being going into the next world but we can also step out here, in this present world. After our loved one dies leaving us in the unknown place, we can know we are being held by God and step out to just begin to live again. Very gradually, I began to do this—with some returning to my "hide-away". I could, perhaps, see a pin-point of light leading me on. Barbara Johnson writes about seeing the light at the end of the tunnel but quotes someone who said "What light? I'm still looking for the tunnel!" ('Pain is inevitable but misery is optional—so stick a geranium in your hat and be happy!'—Barbara Johnson—1990)

I think God can provide us with light all the way through the tunnel as well as just at the end!

Once, I had taken my grandson to the beach and as he held my slippery hand on the edge of the sea his hand came out of mine and he (a toddler) was going in! Simultaneously, I entered the water, with no thought for my clothes or best shoes! Although here the scenario was "grandmother" it showed me my heavenly father was watching over me and would never let me go. I may, in my grief, be behaving as a child but he understood that and was looking after me.

We have times when we can glimpse what He is doing for us through our experiences with people and things down here. I believe we can see glimpses of His love and care in how we love others and how they love us. My love for my grandchild is just a tiny glimpse of His love for us.

He showed me, too, at this time how the awfulness of separation from those loved ones is a small picture of how He feels. He did not want to be separated from us so He sent Jesus to complete the work of salvation. That was the only way He secured a passage for us to always be with Him. Then, for eternity, there will be no separation. I wanted then, as I do now, the King to come back and create His new kingdom that we will be in together. Until that day we will live through the grief with His care and love always with us.

Looking back at my journal, I realise now that God was with me, but sometimes, when the grief and separation were so bad, it didn't feel like it. Even when I started to write this book, I thought I was going to show how my life was empty and how I was not in communication with God. My notes assure me that this was not true. I did hear God speaking and I only got through all of it with Him. I believe, I was closer to Him then than I am now, when my life is getting full of other people and things. If it doesn't feel this way for you, He understands that and you can be real with Him, as I hope I am being with my story here.

Whatever goes on for us, we can know deep inside our hearts that God is there. If you are reading this through your tears of grief know He is there somewhere and one day you will feel His presence again.

Sharing with other people was difficult too. Friends suggested I telephoned whenever I was feeling terrible—"even in the night" they said. It is exceedingly difficult to get out of your chair and, especially out of your bed, and pick up the telephone when you know all you will do is cry down it!

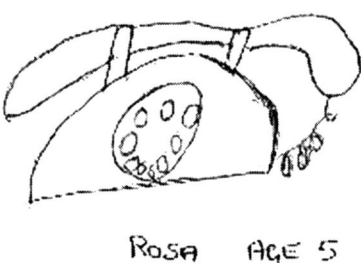

Telephone—by Rosa—aged 5

It was also hard to call on people who told me to do so at anytime. What is better is for someone to say, "Come round for Sunday lunch at 12 o'clock".

I became very sensitive and upset when I felt friends were not inviting me enough. I realise now that I, previously, had not invited people when I could have. I remember being in a car with some people while one of them had a call from her husband and he suggested they got a take-away for supper. I remembered how Allan and I used to do this sometimes on Saturdays and the thought of never doing it again was too much—even like a knife going into my heart. The lady concerned of course didn't know what was going on for me.

Whereas I want you to know what vulnerable feelings go alongside grief I also want to point out how family and friends helped me through. They were wonderful! It was my "broken down" self that didn't always see this at the time.

An entry in my journal—"Oh please someone understand what I am going through". I wanted to tell people the pain was too great but when I was with them I seemed to feel I needed to be alright. Small things appeared gigantic. I had to purchase a new vacuum cleaner but didn't want to do this without Allan as he would have been doing it with me. Many places couldn't be visited as he would have been there. Eating out was definitely not an option, neither were the theatre or cinema. Anything that reminded me of him doing things with me seemed too hard. I felt I would never be happy again. I did! I am!

Heaven was constantly on my mind at this time and one day I asked God "Please tell me something about heaven" He answered, "I have already shown you—LOVE—and there is nothing greater than that." I understood a little because of the love I felt for my husband. God's love of course is so much greater and yet I'm sure He has given us love in this world so we can begin to appreciate and understand His love through our own. I just wanted Allan around all the time. I wonder that Jesus loves me so much that He wants us to be around together all the time!

Just after the first anniversary of Allan's death I remember times of emotionally feeling that maybe I might be happy again. I did feel confused a lot of the time and one day I decided to go for counselling. As a counsellor myself I knew I would encourage anyone else in the same situation to go to one.

Counselling—by Jack—aged 13

The first counsellor I attended started in the very first session to tell me what to do to help myself, for example getting a job. I only went once! Eventually I found one who allowed my grief without telling me how to get over it. She helped me see that I was "in my child" at the moment but that was alright and understandable. She helped me a great deal.

One evening I had what I feel was a revelation that even though confused and grieving I was still "made in the image of God". This was a real blessing to me. He was grieving with me. A great deal of the time I felt I was not handling things very well at all but God was still by my side even if I wasn't at His!

Each morning I woke with a deep longing in my soul to see Allan again. There was an ache in my heart and spirit so much it hurt physically. God loves us like this and longs for us, His people. I took some comfort from the book of Psalms. David was real about his depressed state and much sorrow which he expressed. He also trusted in 'God's unfailing love'. (Psalm 13 NLT) I tried to do this. David was called "a man after my own heart" by God and yet he was down so much of the time.

Once I had a picture of a shepherd with a lamb across his shoulders. There nothing could touch it and it was safe from the dangerous path below. Here we can rest on our great shepherd, hear His voice and be carried until our broken hearts are mended. Here we can recover and when He puts us down we will know what to do.

Turning Points

About eighteen months after Allan's death, I managed to make a trip to Kenya. I had been before, with Allan, and our lives were never the same again; after seeing street kids, orphaned babies rescued from rubbish dumps, and much deep poverty. Although difficult to go without my husband, it turned out to be the first turning point in my grief. Some of this, I feel, was because of experiencing the poverty I have mentioned. Also some help came from seeing Christians with constant faith in a comforting God who was actually in control. They worshipped and were so thankful for the fact that they were going to eternity. The thought of seeing and being with Jesus was what kept them going. Most of them would die well before sixty-one (the age of my husband when he died). The conditions of their living left much to be desired; they knew what it meant to live for God alone.

On my journey home, while bumping over many pot-holes in a large vehicle called a matatu that looked and felt as if it was falling apart, I couldn't help but listen to the very loud music the driver played. I think the loud-speaker was the part of the vehicle that apparently was working the best of all its various parts! I listened first to a song about how God heals. As He had not managed to heal my husband I felt He did not heal anymore. The song that followed was "God will make a way when there seems to be no way". (Don Meon)

My son and daughter-in-law had given me a card with the same words on it. I pondered whether or not He could actually make a way for me to live again. Through many tears, I seemed to hear God whisper to my heart, "I can and I will." It is hard to explain what took place in my heart that moment but something did. Although I didn't have an answer for the "why" of Allan's death, I began to know and accept that God was still God. I still don't have the answer but I do know God is the healer still. I began from that moment to believe He was, and is, and always will be everything to me. I started ever so slightly to believe that God could and would make a way for me to live again.

On returning home I would play the song "making a way" over and over again. I couldn't sing along with it at this stage but got comfort from this song booming out as loud as it would go. Music seems to heal even when we can't join in! I felt closer to God than ever before but was still unable to completely trust Him about the future. There seemed to be a paradox in my life—I wanted to enjoy my time on this earth and yet I wanted to go to heaven. I felt He told me that was alright!

I loved Allan so deeply and I wanted to be able to love God like that. I realised God wants our love so much He looks at us like we look at one another when first in love! I knew He was doing this all through my grief—even at my worst doubting times. God longs for us so much—more than I was longing for Allan! In my weak sorrowful state God spoke to me and comforted me. Just when I thought I was unable to go on, He would drop something into my heart which carried me a little further.

In the book of Job, with all the dreadful things going on in Job's life, he spoke these words, "I know that my Redeemer lives" (Job 19:25 NLT) I knew Jesus wanted my love and I began to think I could give this to Him.

Two years on in my bereavement I attended a conference (Association of Christian Counsellors) and someone, I had not previously met, chatted with me and had a picture in their mind for me and my situation. They told me about a kaleidoscope with a pattern that changes if it gets knocked. The pattern does not return to the same one but another one, equally as beautiful, emerges.

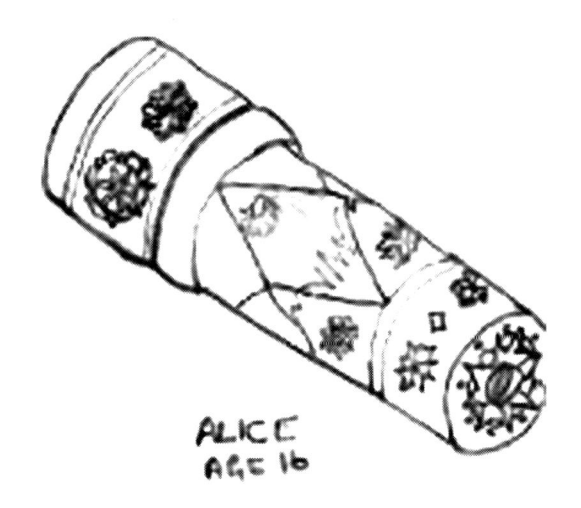

Kaleidoscope—by Alice—aged 16

My life had been knocked and the pattern changed forever but a new one had appeared. This was a wonderful thought and it remained with me, although at times, I still could feel my broken heart. The crack in it has been mended now but the scar is still there and as some memory brushes alongside it, discomfort is still felt.

Driving one day on a familiar route, the usually wonderful view was shrouded in mist. I knew the view was still there even though I couldn't see it. When next time I travelled this road, when the mist had lifted, I would see the view perfectly. My grief was still occasionally keeping the view from me—or the kaleidoscope pattern—but soon it would lift and I would see clearly. Beautiful thoughts like these were such a comfort to me as I walked the path of life mapped out for me. Could I see a light at the end of the tunnel? I believe I could.

Over the next few months I gradually felt the mist lifting. I didn't cry so often and my emotions became steadier. I began to enjoy—yes enjoy—things and feel warmth in some memories, as well as the sadness. I remember well the first time I felt the wind on my face and liking it. I could go for a walk on my own and enjoy it. My home was again a comforting place.

Saturday evenings had been tremendously difficult as this was the time we sat and enjoyed things together. I have a clear memory of going to the fish and chip shop and for the first time plucking up the courage to ask for ONE portion of chips! I did drink quite a lot of cider to go with the portion. I still often felt lonely but not in such a bitter way.

The phase of anger did not pass me by either. I shouted at God occasionally to ask why He took Allan from me. I knew He was big enough to cope with that! I believe in a God who knows the 'stages of grief' very well!

If you are reading this while grieving, please allow yourself to go through at your own pace. It will not be the same as mine. Remember—"It doesn't come to stay it comes to pass!" (Barbara Johnson 1990)

I hope you can take some of my experiences and know at least someone else has been devastated in grief beyond despair and yet has arrived at a better place.

"It will be alright in the morning/mourning"—yes it will! If you are not there yet, please try to believe it will get better and better as it has for me. I can still miss him deeply sometimes but I am also living a very full, happy life.

It has taken a very long time for me to put this story together. I have drawn mostly on my journal entries. I have now married again—but that's another story!

I hope and pray that someone has found strength and hope through my ramblings. Remember—"It will be alright in the morning/mourning!"

"And now I want you to know what happens to a Christian when he dies so that when it happens you will not be full of sorrow as those who have no hope. For since we believe that Jesus died and then came back to life again we can also believe that when Jesus returns God will bring back with Him all the Christians who have died . . . For the Lord Himself will come down from heaven with a mighty shout and with the soul stirring cry of the archangel and the great trumpet call of God. The believers who are dead will be the first to rise and meet the Lord. Then we who are still alive and remain on the earth will be caught up with them in the clouds to meet the Lord in the air and remain with Him forever. So comfort and encourage each another with this news." (1 Thessalonians 4:13-18 TLB)

PART TWO

I do hope you have already read the account of my grieving. I suspect if you have, many thoughts and feelings of your own have been evoked, and you probably have mapped out the way you could have helped me, had I had the pleasure of finding you as my counsellor!

Let me declare here and now that having been a counsellor myself for many years and having made many mistakes, I don't intend the following to be a formula for therapists. I believe the individual grieving process is different for everyone and therefore any help received will be different too. It is with this in mind that I only want to put forward some thoughts and ideas which may be helpful while you seek to help others. Certainly do not try to put these in order all the time or even any of the time. As with any other counselling process, we need the theory or model in the back of our minds, drawing on them as and when appropriate.

If I have to declare my orientation, I would say the client is the expert and I, the counsellor, am there for them alone. This would be called "person-centred" and, given the right environment, I trust the client to find the answers for themselves and in their time.

I adhere to the approach that the most important part of counselling is the relationship between the client and the counsellor. In his book, "Forms of Feeling", Robert Hobson explains it like this "Problems in personal relationships cannot be resolved by talking about them, by explaining them from outside. They can only be explored and tackled effectively in the experience of being within a relationship". (Hobson 1987)

His "Conversational Method" seems to have some alignment with the person-centred approach. If you are going to walk alongside a grieving person, ask yourself, firstly, if you can be fully present with them in their grief and all that will mean. Reading my story may help you decide if you are in a place to be able to do this.

Of course no counsellor is perfect so if at any time through the process of counselling you are aware of your own emotions it may be appropriate to show congruence, letting the client in on yourself and your own place at the time. Always be sure, when self-disclosing, that you are doing it for the client and not for your own benefit.

Being fully present with the client will mean you offer unconditional positive regard and acceptance—not allowing any judgmental attitude of yours to creep in. Never let there be a time of limiting the grief, tears or other emotions. The deepest empathy you can give will allow the client to understand your acceptance of them and all they are bringing, and this realisation may help them accept all they feel at this time.

If you show them they are completely acceptable, they can begin to believe this about themselves and realise a peace of mind regarding the process they are going through.

A word of warning that as you try to walk alongside it is not helpful to say, "I completely understand what you are going through" because you do not! Even if you have grieved, the process will not be exactly the same.

I am aware that I have used phrases that may not be understood by counsellors of orientations other than that of the person-centred approach. However, I do not want to elaborate on these here but if further understanding is required I suggest reading "Person-centred Counselling in Action". Here Dave Mearns and Brian Thorne describe the approach and give insight in an easy to understand way. (Mears & Thorne 1999)

Whilst recognising there are stages of grief I don't believe they always go in the "right order"—whatever that might be! Usually the shock of death is present at the beginning but may last for any amount of time. Even if there has been illness or something that indicated the person close was going to die, the shock of them not being there is still prevalent. It is around this time we may be asked to stand alongside someone and, if so, be prepared for anything.

I personally went away from the hospital bed quite calmly thinking I just had to go home. I sometimes ignored people who had come to comfort me as, if I acknowledged their caring, I was admitting the loved one had gone. Alongside this attitude I did not want to be left alone. I went from screaming that it could not be happening to sobbing for hours that it had. I drew so much on family and their presence and yet I wanted to leave this world and go to heaven to be with my husband.

I needed someone to listen and be there for me with all the various emotions and desperate thoughts and not to judge me. We often do and say things we don't mean while grieving and in my own experience, that lasted a very long time. I didn't want helpful suggestions. I only wanted to pour out whatever I wanted to and for someone to say that was alright. So to be able to listen, and stay with the emotions that are emerging, is probably the most important skill in 'counselling' the bereaved. Of course this needs to be without judging, otherwise, it will do more harm than good. Family and friends cannot always do this for whatever reason, and so to know you can regularly be with someone who will, is exceedingly helpful and healing. I hesitate to move on from this as the listening, 'staying with' and not judging should always be there throughout counselling.

In an interview for "The Psychologist", Darian Leader says:

> "Mourning doesn't have such neat stages. It's a very complicated thing. It takes a long time and it can also never happen". (Article by Renee Lertzman)

I think when he uses the phrase "never happen" he is suggesting that sometimes it's much easier not to mourn as it is too painful. The griever is not engaging with the loss. Denying the loss is therefore the soft option.

I use this quote to emphasise the absence of stages in mourning. I, therefore, am not attempting to suggest stages but am now going to put forward various emotions and thoughts that will probably come up somewhere in the process of grieving.

"In Denial"

This is an expression we hear said about those who are grieving. Sometimes it can be spoken in a condemning way and even with scorn or derision. It cannot be helped! There may be a mixture of denying the loved one has gone and then also living in reality. Fantasy worlds are often invented. Living as though the person is still there with us is very common. In whatever way this is done, you should respect it.

The shock of a death of someone close to a client may have a profound affect on them. The ability to cope and to really assimilate what has happened may be too overwhelming and therefore the person finds themselves in denial. If this didn't happen, emotional and physical issues would be just too much to bear.

Hopefully, as counsellors we allow our clients to bring experiences into the room which are beyond our own, allowing them to speak of anything they wish to. Don't make the mistake of thinking bereavement is in any way a lesser issue than other traumatic experiences. We need to extend the same level of empathy to all clients who will often talk of things which are difficult for us to hear. We need to accept whatever fantasy that is brought into the counselling room. We may find our client brings their loved one into the room as well as themselves, speaking of them as though they were still alive and on this earth. Be prepared to be open enough to listen well.

As a counsellor just starting out, I learnt the hard way; a young lady came for counselling just after her mother had died. Among other things she told me how she didn't want to move anything that had belonged to her mother, wanting it to be just as she had left it. Clearly she wanted her mother to still be in her room. She spoke of her mother's handbag being there and after listening for a while, I suggested that she might move the handbag (probably the most personal thing there). I was trying to help but only how I thought it would help. Needless to say, she didn't return for further sessions!

I would like to consider here, the way other cultures deal with grief, particularly looking at the expression of emotions. It would appear at first that some cultures are never in denial, in that they encourage much expression of feeling. In certain African and Asian cultures, it is common at the death of a loved one, to weep loudly in public with other relations and friends accompanying. In the culture I am used to, it is supposed that crying will be done on our own and quietly. However, I did weep all the way through my husbands funeral, albeit quietly.

It has been said that cultures that mourn publicly are greatly helped by this behaviour. Canon Dr. Bill Merington writes of his visits to Africa and Asia, when he was trying to discover how culture affects our grieving. He found, mostly, that over-loudly expressed feelings did not have much positive influence on the process of grief in the long run. As time went on, mourners showed signs of great loss, in a similar way to that of his own culture. He writes, "They showed daily recall and ongoing rumination with emotions close to the surface. There was holding on to possessions of the deceased, a general feeling of isolation in the community and regular visiting of the grave". (Accord magazine issue 73)

Everyone has their own way of dealing with grief and we definitely need to go along with their way. We must be extremely sensitive to the emotions, thoughts and fantasies of the person sitting in front of us. We can enter into their world, but only as much as they want us to. Some thoughts and things will be so personal they will want to keep them so.

Talking to the loved one is very common. It is another way of keeping them with us. I found myself doing this a great deal, and worried about what I was doing. Having been brought up to believe very strongly that trying to contact the dead was exceedingly wrong, (of course I wasn't doing this), it bothered me that I was speaking out loud to my husband. Ask yourself if you have ever spoken audibly to a partner, child or friend who happens to be late coming home or is not doing what we wish they would! They are not within hearing range but we speak as if they are. Someone has been part of our life and it still feels as if they are and this is very much the desire of our hearts.

So, be careful about the phrase "in denial". The bereaved will need time to adjust to the fact that their loved one is not around, and that will be as long as it takes!

Guilt

The area of guilt can show up in many forms; more often than not it raises its extremely ugly head when a person is mourning. How many times do we hear 'I feel I could have done more—in the relationship, in the time left together, the way I was handling things, the words I spoke or not, to prevent the death, I should have seen signs, I should have sent him to the doctor sooner'?

We can spend so much time in guilt trying to repay the deceased in some way. We cannot necessarily get rid of guilt by telling the person they are not guilty. I once tried to help a man who had lost his partner six years previously. He said he was guilty because he did not persuade her to have the treatment offered to her at the time. She didn't want anything other than natural treatment. Still, six years on, the guilt remained. He told me he just had to live with it. The guilt felt needs to be explored but only when the grieving one is ready. They may want to hang on to their story—including guilt—as this keeps a link to the past. Only when the person sitting in front of you is ready, and only then, can guilt be explored.

As an aside for a moment, but illustrating dealing with the feeling of guilt, I want to share something that happened in my past. I did something wrong which involved other people. I wanted to feel right about it and be forgiven. For a while, I put the blame on my counsellor as I felt I was led astray by him. However, it was only when I admitted the wrong part I played in the scenario, that I was able to feel forgiven by God, others and myself! I could not be forgiven for that which I hadn't done but admitting the part I had was essential. I cannot be guilty for murdering my neighbour because I haven't done it and so therefore I cannot be forgiven for it!

There are two ways of getting rid of guilt—either by knowing fully that we did not do wrong or by admitting our wrong and being forgiven. There may be something that grieving people really believe they could have done differently and needed to have addressed before parting from their loved ones. They may need to admit this and accept forgiveness from God and their loved one (who is now perfect and ready to forgive) and then also forgive themselves. Your own attitude can help. This may be a way of getting rid of the feeling of guilt.

There may be guilt that is peculiar to Christians who believe they should not be grieving at all if they trust God! 1 Thessalonians 4:13 (NLT) states "you will not grieve like people who have no hope." The meaning here is that we will see the dead person again and so we can be comforted by that. Of course this is true but it does not say "you will not grieve!" No one should feel guilty with the feelings of grief they have.

I want to stress again that, as a counsellor, this exploration should only occur as the client feels happy about it. If the subject of guilt has raised its ugly head, and as you gently attempt to open the grieving eyes to another way, only continue down this path in a place of peace for both the client and you. If I had my way, I would wish you, the reader, and your clients to have such a picture of God's love that it surpasses all guilt. It's not my way that matters, or your way, but the clients.

Anger

Depression can often be thought of as repressed anger. So many times a person can keep a lid on their anger because the belief is that it is wrong to be angry. This can come about because of our "conditions of worth" when we were told we must not be angry or some such thing. We internalised the notion that, in order to be accepted, our angry feelings need to be suppressed.

Therapists who adhere to "attachment theories" purport that anger, which accompanies grief, can often be linked with childhood when the infant feels they are losing their mother. The child will feel abandoned and rejected.

Similar feelings of abandonment and rejection can be felt when we lose a loved one. The grieving one may show anger towards the person they feel has left them, or they may have the anger but not allow it to surface as the rational part of them knows that person could do nothing to stop the separation.

A child may ignore a loved parent when they return from, even a short, stay away being a reaction to abandonment. Does this occur when a loved one leaves in the act of dying? It may be that grief causes a similar reaction and the grieving person may not want to think or talk of their departed one, almost as a defiant anger towards them.

Their anger can be directed towards others. Sometimes this can be medical staff, family and friends, God or even themselves. We hear clients talking about how they could have done more to prevent the death of the loved one. Anger can also be revealed in the form of irritability. Frustration may come as they just simply cannot be bothered with other people around them. Whatever the form, you as the counsellor need to treat it, as you do all other emotions, with acceptance and not judgment.

As stated at the beginning of this paragraph, if anger is not allowed in a safe environment, severe depression can set in for a long time, and even bitterness, prolonging or deepening the grieving process.

Loneliness

Loneliness would normally be a negative feeling. Being alone is not the same; it can be very positive especially when wanting to write a manuscript! Loneliness that comes alongside bereavement can be very difficult to express. It is extremely hard to actually say to another person—however close we are to them—"I am lonely". Guilt can raise its ugly head again and we may feel ashamed that we feel this way. It is easy to imagine that no one else feels this way about life.

A great deal is said these days about how we need to be positive. Introvert personalities can believe themselves to be "worse" than the extroverts, who may appear to be always positive! Loneliness can of course merge across these two extremes but I am just commenting on how devastatingly awful aloneness can feel.

As hard as it may be for clients to express their loneliness in the counselling room, please be unconditionally accepting. This can possibly bring them to accept their own feelings and even to accept, in time, that loneliness is sometimes around for all of us.

In my own grief, I felt I had no one to put me first, now my partner was gone. I knew others loved me but I was not the primary one in another's life. Fear may creep in here as well. We may have anxiety about the future and facing it on our own. It may seem that what is now, will always be, which of course is not necessarily the case. We can also be afraid of loving other people in case we lose them too and this causes more loneliness as we withdraw into ourselves further. This can also apply to the counsellor. The client fails to disclose much of themselves as you, the counsellor, might leave them as well. Loneliness is regarded as the main reason for suicide attempts. Much care is needed here and possibly communication about how the counsellee is feeling.

I believe I should refer here to the "tenderness" that Brian Thorne suggests is something to be brought into the counselling room with much benefit to the client. He writes, "When I am bold enough to accept my own uniqueness it seems that I am enabled to offer a tenderness which moves the soul while embracing (sometimes literally) the body." (Person-centred Counselling in Action 1999) Can we as counsellors be open and courageous enough to offer lonely, grieving people our tenderness?

When addressing the subject of loneliness in his book "Forms of Feeling" Robert Hobson describes "Moments of Meeting" in which, if tenderness crosses over from one person to another, "a gap" becomes closed between them. (Hobson 1987)

Dreaming

Dreaming and remembering the dreams is prevalent at the time of grief. The client may bring them up in a session and, especially, if the person who has died appears in them. Some analysts may want to interpret these but, from my point of view, and, for that matter, from a person-centred view, the client is the important analyst here.

Allowing the dreams to be explored can be an important part of grieving. Pay particular attention to any feelings that come up either in the dream itself or on waking and also the emotions in the counselling room. While the dream is being recounted, listen carefully to emotive words that are used during this process. Feeding back to the person can often allow them to experience the dream again and discover what it is really about.

Recurring dreams are particularly significant. For a time I used to dream I was in a group or meeting and although I had arrived with my husband I could not find him when I needed him. He appeared to be lost from me. Sometimes I found him but, when I did, he would not communicate with me. I would wake with the grieving emotions. This recurring dream may appear to have obvious connotations. However, as I acknowledged the thoughts and feelings either to another person, or sometimes writing them down, it gradually helped to dispel things that were present for me in my grief. For me, and this is not always the case, I found "unfinished business" raising its head in my dreaming. I needed to confront this but only when ready to do so. The process was painful. So, as with anything else, stay with the person and their grief until they are ready to let the process move on.

Dreams can be another way of holding onto the person who has left. Even if pain is involved in the dreaming, it still can allow a feeling of closeness to the person rather than not having them at all. The memory of them is a very precious thing.

My granddaughter quite recently was crying as she looked at a photo of grandpa. She told me "I am afraid I can't remember grandpa anymore!" She didn't like that thought. We want to remember so much but even that is painful at the beginning. I was told by well-meaning friends to remember the good things which I couldn't do at first as everything seemed too bad! I can do this now and it helps me a great deal. Wanting memories is desirable but they can be painful; painful if we do remember but also if we don't!

Really our family and friends "can't win" as everything that is done and said hurts. The person—you the counsellor—who listens to everything non-judgmentally, may be the only hope at this stage.

Feeling Sorry for Oneself

This feeling is very normal but, can obviously, be hard for family or friends to live with. If we have lost the dearest person on earth it is quite natural for us to be feeling this way. We surely had dreams and aspirations that would happen with us and the lost one. Now we feel we have to face the future alone. The disappointment at that time may be unbearable.

I remember many occasions when I expected friends to be there for me just whenever I wished them to be and being extremely upset if they had something else to do!

These emotions can also cause the grieving one to become, or want to become, so attached to a counsellor that it is difficult not to be dependent on that relationship. This may happen for a while but, of course, as a counsellor we cannot be spending our time only with one client to make them feel better. However, when we are there for them in a regular meeting we can be a 'rock' for them. They can gradually learn, and be able to know, they will be alright on their own moving from that 'rock' as and when they can. A regular slot can help to ease their pain. To have something to look forward to, say once a week, can be a beginning of "looking forward" for them.

We may, as counselors, become overwhelmed with a client, especially one with so much need. Of course we would never tell them to "get over it" or "pull themselves together" but there can be feelings of this nature within us so we should be aware of ourselves and congruently deal with our situation. We can always let our emotions out with our supervisor. Self disclosure may be necessary but make sure the person sitting in front of you is able to cope with your disclosure, checking it out with them as you go along. Ask yourself, "Am I doing this for the client's well-being or am I really doing it for me!"

If your client is a Christian, with access to a bible, the following verse may help them:

> "After you have suffered a little while our God who is full of kindness through Christ will give you His eternal glory. He personally will come and pick you up and set you firmly in place and make you stronger than ever." (1 Peter 5:10: TLB)

A Lack of Confidence

A lack of confidence, which may not have been known, before can descend. The world that has been experienced up to the point of loss is now upside-down and, therefore, appears to be completely strange. Everything, at one level, goes on just as before—but nothing is the same! The journey through grief has to be done but the path is not known. Therefore, the grief is causing us to walk, rather stumble, through a way which makes us feel inadequate and hopeless. I remember driving to church and sitting in my car, in the car park, trying to work out how I could walk into the church. Having been to church many times before—this time was different. To go in on my own was a new experience. In these situations we can feel like a child again. Getting to a supermarket was different too. Going for a walk on my own was completely out of the question.

Many fears can raise their ugly heads. These can be the fear of not being able to cope in the present or the fear of what might happen in the future. We don't know how long we may have to be on our own or what may have to be faced. Being able to talk things over with a partner is not available anymore. This, of course, may be where the counsellor comes in and again I ask you to realise how important a listening ear is.

The trauma of grief can cause people to have panic attacks. They may never have experienced such before but feeling weak and vulnerable, and being in situations that have not been around before, causes someone to feel they do not know how to behave or conduct themselves.

When a partner dies there can be many things, jobs or knowledge that have never been contemplated before by the one that is left. These may be such things as cooking and housework or gardening, accounts and many others. I did not know how to fill the car up with petrol or even work the TV.!

Not knowing what to do in situations will often provide fuel for a lack of confidence. Dependence on another person is not realised often until we are left on our own. We can ask ourselves, as therapists, what we would be like on our own.

Isolation may breed a lack of confidence. The weekly visit to the counsellor can be the only outing a person has for a while as they seek to open up to a new way of living.

One book and author that helped my grieving was "A Grief Observed" by C. S. Lewis. He wrote this after the death of his wife. He says, "For in grief nothing stays put. One keeps on emerging from a phase, but it always recurs. Round and round. Everything repeats." (Lewis 1978). Lewis was a confident intelligent writer but his book shows how grieving affected him so he certainly did not seem confident.

To read about grief from someone who has been on the path can be very reassuring. Although you, as the counsellor, may not have experienced the same path it will be comforting for the person sitting in front of you to have some company as they tread the way they have to go. The lack of confidence is there as we have not walked that way before. A sense of their own amazing worth will grow as you believe in their worth and communicate that to them in words, tenderness and love.

Physical Changes

I should mention that physical changes can be experienced as well as emotional ones. We are "whole" people. The physical body has links with our emotional state. Many physicians believe most illnesses have their roots in a person's stresses and emotions.

Palpitations are common when people are going through a stressful time. I believe these are not necessarily dangerous and will leave as quickly as they came. However, occasionally the heart can give much more serious symptoms and the stress of grief may even cause a heart attack. Recent research has shown heart attacks among people who have been bereaved are more likely within the first few months. These are usually, though, in those who have shown symptoms previously. It certainly does put a new meaning to the phrase "dying of a broken heart".

The most obvious physical symptom is a great deal of crying!

Headaches may be common especially if sleep is disturbed. Often the person falls asleep fairly well but wakes at a ridiculously early time. Other aches and pains are likely as well.

There can be a loss of appetite or the reverse. Comfort eating is very common. When I was first bereaved I would visit a store and, after buying two cream cakes, would sit in the car eat one and then eat the other as soon as returning home! It did amaze me that I still lost weight as I just ate all I wished for. Weight loss, apparently, is common. Nausea is also something that is frequently experienced.

A tightening of the throat, causing discomfort, is common. I found I had a lack of concentration when first bereaved. It seemed to go after a while. I hope this is the case for your clients otherwise they won't be able to read my book!

Our immune system can take a bashing and, therefore, we may be susceptible to illness.

If it is felt to be manageable, exercise is very beneficial, but there will probably be times of feeling extremely lethargic and, as the process of grieving takes its toll, there will be physical exhaustion.

It is also noted that, if a person does not allow themselves to grieve, often physical problems will raise their ugly heads much later in life.

I am not medically trained so want to be careful about mentioning things that may not be relevant to the grieving process at all.

Indeed, some of the above may not always be present. As a counsellor, check the client is seeing his or her doctor—a very wise thing to do.

Hope

There may be things you will discover on your journey with your client that I have not mentioned. As you stay alongside empathically listening, whatever comes on the path can appear manageable and less daunting with you there.

The counsellor offers such an important role but I hesitate to use the word *role* as this is not role-play but real life. You may never know the extent to which you have aided the person to walk through their grief. Allow me to encourage you to tread alongside—not in front or behind—and, in this way, to ease the burden of the sufferer.

I began my thoughts, at the outset of this book, suggesting there is a "going through" of grief. I believe I have personally done just that. It seemed to be an exceedingly long and tiresome path and the tunnel was dark at times. However, now I can look back and realise there was light and comfort just for the asking. I do have faith that it was God who helped me through. The writings of my journal support this notion, and I trust you and your clients experience an undying unconditional love too.

I have learnt, through my experiences, many things which, I am sure, help me to live life to the full now. Whatever happens in the future will also be coloured by having walked this way and makes me feel nothing is ever too hard to "go through!"

Ecclesiastes 3:4 (NLT) says, "A time to grieve and a time to dance!" Let's hope your clients find both. In the mourning/morning may they dance!

Bibliography

Hobson, Robert, "Forms of Feeling" The Heart of Psychotherapy, New York/London: Tavistock/Routledge, 1985.

Johnson, Barbara, "Pain is inevitable but misery is optional", USA: W. Publishing Group, 1990.

Lertzman, Renee, Interview with Leader, The Psychologist British Psychological Society, 2011.

Lewis, C.S., "A Grief Observed", London/Boston: Faber and Faber Paperbacks, 1978.

Mearns, Dave and Brian Thorne, "Person-centred Counselling in Action", London: Sage Publications, 1988.

Merrington, Bill, "Cultural Affect when a Child Dies", Issue 73, Accord Magazine-Association of Christian Counsellors, 2011/12.

Paterson Smyth, J. (Fortieth British edition), "The Gospel of the Hereafter", London: Hodder and Stoughton Ltd.

Song "God will make a way" Don Meon.

Biblical References are all taken from "The Living Bible" (TLB) and "New Living Translation" (NLT).

CPSIA information can be obtained at www.ICGtesting.com
Printed in the USA
BVOW072319061112

304867BV00001B/5/P